*Wayne Dyer, ﹏
Lama, Albert E﹏
Buddha, Khalil Gibran, Nikola
Tesla, Robert Kiyosaki, Dolores
Cannon, Jesus Christ, Justin Bieber
and more*
share their wisdom:

# Pearls of the Genius

Sascha Të Light & Nino Anders

Freiheit. JETZT!

Nino Anders
Papyrus Autoren-Club
R.O.M. Logicware GmbH
Pettenkoferstr. 16-18
10247 Berlin

ISBN-13: 9798566396644

In eternal gratitude for your feedback/your
opinion/your review:

https://www.amazon.com/dp/B08NRL
JBRX

# The table of contents

# Categorie Water, Diet and Knowledge

# Categorie Finances

# Categorie Wisdom

# The Digression of Happiness

# Enlightenment

This book is a combination of stories and aphorisms about life. The aphorisms communicate the most valuable and inspiring thoughts of the most prominent people and traditions of human history.

Read this book slowly, sometimes only one page a day, to be fully reborn after your completion with a deep understanding and implementation of enlightening ideas.

One idea is enough to completely revolutionize your life, because

*"Nothing is as strong as an idea whose time has come."*

# Twofold Introduction

I was sitting in my car in Moruya, Australia, thinking about life. In a form of deep meditation and trance, I enjoyed the moment of silence and allowed the source of being to give me deep insights. I knew that this moment was a different one, because my inner voice prepared me cheerfully. Slowly, word for word, the voice revealed the following insight to me:

The


following

words

are

going to

change

your

life

fundamentally.

"Yes! Great!" I thought, full of anticipation and excitement. And they were:

# I

**am**

# completely

free,

# from

**the**

# Inside

**out,**

# NOW!

I am completely free, from the Inside out, NOW!

This they are. And the anticipation was not too much of a promise. I felt overwhelmed by the profound insight. Freedom, the most sacred ideal I am striving for, which I deeply love. Freedom, perfect freedom, the highest good in life and being. Pure, perfect freedom. Given to me, in this moment. I felt deep gratitude to have become worthy of being granted with this idea. Ideas, the true gods of creation. Capable to revolutionize life from one instance to another fundamentally. At the beginning of everything is the thought, second is the feeling of this thought and what this is capable of and can imply. Pictures and visions drawn in color emerge further out of this realization into a new way of living.

I am completely free, from the Inside out, NOW!

I knew straight away, I had to share these words. With all the people of the world who feel the call to receive them. In this way, dear reader, God has led you here, to read these words. We are all connected and I am here as a channel, to earn the highest insights to life for the reason of sharing them with you. It is for you that I live, life is the service to one's neighbour. Frequently have I been thinking about the following questions, which I can imagine that you already had them as well:

How can I inspire as many people as positively as possible?

How can I be the best possible present to humanity?

And this is how the words "I am completely free, from the Inside out, NOW!" transpired to:

We are completely free, from the Inside out, NOW!

Just imagine, you are very welcome to do that regularly, what exactly this implies to you. How does this realization, the fruition of this idea feel to you? What does perfect freedom mean — to you, for your life, and the life of all? Perfect freedom. Most sacred good, supreme ideal - See it as being realized now and it is yours.

In order to make this idea more comprehensible and to support the fruition of it effectively, the "Pearls of the Genius" are shared with you here now. These pearls allow to look at life in a way to understand what Wayne Dyer understood:

"Heaven on Earth is not a place, it is a decision."

Living in complete freedom for everyone, NOW.

We are Love, We are Light, We are free. We are beautiful -

Sascha Të Light.

This first episode was one starting point for this book. The second one appeared through a meeting. I met a special person in Thessaloniki. Thessaloniki, a wonderful place located in beautiful Greece, Macedonia with a long and great history. It is also very close to Mount Olympus.

The special person is called Tonino and we understood each other instantly. Similar habits and mutual respect were present from the very beginning. We stayed in contact for a long time beyond our first meeting in Thessaloniki. Tonino felt admiration that I was able to organize, structure and focus my thoughts to write books. Throughout his life, he had gathered a collection of aphorisms, to which he regularly turns, "Every day," he once told me. He shared them with me and I found them just as enlightening and was instantly on fire to share them in the form of a book. However, it took some time for this book to be born into publicity. May your quality of life flourish with the support of this collection of ideas.

Here are the aphorisms of wisdom, allow them stimulate you, read gladly one each day, and think about them for longer, what they mean, what they stand for. Thoughts are the beginning, let these thoughts emerge and create your life with a deep sense of understanding, streaked with multifarious images and visions in your imagination, which resemble the words of Wayne Dyer and Sascha Të Light:

Heaven on Earth, in complete freedom, NOW!


In Love,

Nino Anders

# Categorie God

… because God is, what we all are.

Why within you

Nourish the fire of your longing, increase your desire for freedom until only that is left. And say yes, say yes to everything that happens, whether pleasant or unpleasant! Say yes to you; you are created exactly as you are! You are an expression of the Divine as you are - with all your nooks and crannies! I can only see divinity in you. You are the same self as I am, and I see Buddha in every being. That is why I see God in you too!

Pyar Troll

Eternal

The whole creation exists in you, and all that is in you also exists in creation. There is a connection between you and an object that is very close to you, just as there is a connection between you and very distant objects. All things, the smallest and largest, the lowest and highest are present in you as equal. A single atom contains all the elements of the earth. A single movement of the Spirit implies all the laws of life.

Khalil Gibran

Branches of the same tree

All religions, arts, philosophies and sciences are like branches of the same tree. All these efforts are aimed at refining human life, lifting it out of the sphere of a merely vital existence and leading the individual to inner liberation.


Albert Einstein

Jesus said (about the essence of God)

I am the light that is above all. I am the universe. The universe has come out of me and the universe has come back to me. Split a piece of wood, and I am there. Lift a stone, and you will find me there.

Jesus Christ

God lives within you

Everything unfolds as it should. Be honest with yourself and the right things will happen in your life. Remember to love yourself, to worship yourself, to pray to yourself, to bow down to yourself. For God lives in you as YOU!

Robert Adams

To know the starting point

We will continue to search, and at the end of our search we will get back to where we started. However, for the first time we will really know our starting point.

T.S. Eliot

## Perfect Buddha-being

Our original Buddha being is, from the standpoint of the highest truth, empty, omnipresent, silent and pure. It is glorious and mysterious joy. Penetrate deep into it by waking up yourself. You can study everything and at the end of all of your studies you will come to realize, that what you have in front of you at every moment is this Buddha being in all its perfection, which has always been here with you.

Huang Po

Interest

Interest is God's highest virtue. God loves to know and experience everything. The lived interest in the conditions of others is God's way of life. Live like God. Be curious.

Dolores Cannon

## You are everything

Claim back your strength! Forget all the nonsense about the mind and the body and the thoughts and the world and God and everything else that seems to be real. Do not compare yourself to anyone. Be honest with yourself. It does not matter how advanced someone else may be. Forget all saints and sages and other people. You are the only one that has ever existed, and you are the only one that exists. You are all saints and all wise men and all seers. You are everything. Wake up! Why do you want to play games with yourself for so long? By believing in reincarnation, you come over and over again, always hoping for a better next life. Now is the only life.

Robert Adams

God loves me.

It always watches over me. It is always there. It always knows what I do and it always supports with the most instructive experiences. I trust it. I trust that everything, every decision, every idea in my mind is in natural perfect harmony with the task, the message, the intention of my being, which is why the source, God, has created me, in love.

Sascha Të Light

Eternal "I am".

When I advance to the depths of my own existence and my own present reality, the indefinable "Being" which represents my self in its deepest roots and then penetrate through this deep center, then I find myself in the infinite "I am", which is the name of God.

Thomas Merton

The Kingdom of God.

His disciples said to Jesus: "The kingdom, when will it come?" The kingdom of the Father has already spread over the earth. Open your eyes and you will recognize it.

Jesus Christ

It is the same with the awakening.

It seems like you are looking at the world "out there", which seems very real, as if it were separate from you. But suddenly you realize - you just realize that you are just looking at your own self and that your self is the whole world as it arises from moment to moment, right now and now and now. When you become a witness to the world, the world arises in the witness and you and the world are one. You are heaven. You are the song of the birds. You are the earth. All this comes in a sudden, spontaneous, realization. The realization of the "one taste", your original self, your original face that you had before your parents were born, the self you had before the universe was born; this pure, omnipresent, perfect self, beyond the space and eternal; and yet it is the only one you have ever known. You already know that you are this self; and this self is in the truest sense of the word pure spirit.

Ken Wilber

Life is experience – the observation of small dreams in larger dreams.

What is the difference between falling asleep and dying? Both are followed by the birth, of a new day, of a new lifetime. Days, such as lifetimes are small dreams within bigger dreams. What does this mean for us today, now? Simply to be in the Now. Just to enjoy, to observe, to be and this forever, in the Now.

Robert Adams

To live in the NOW.

Do not run after the past. Do not lose yourself in the future. The past is no longer. The future has not yet come. Life is here and now.

Lao Tzu

# SAI BABA

One warm summer day, I sat on a bench in front of my hotel in Ipoh, Malaysia. I ate my nuts, which I rewarded myself with for my previously finished writings.

An elderly man came along the street. I was surprised when he sat down next to me on the bench and started talking. He asked me about my name, where I was coming from and how I like Malaysia and Ipoh so far. After a while, he said I was different. Unlike ordinary tourists. Many come here because of the cheap lifestyle, the cheap food, the warm climate and the sex. He saw my big eyes and said **"Yees, sex is a core part to life!"**

Rarely that you talk to a stranger about sex just after five minutes of knowing. He said I dress differently, I talk differently, I would be special.

I liked the man. Of course, he gave me appreciation in this way. **Giving sincere appreciation is the key to the hearts of all.**

Inspired by this, I said that I actually practice some "unusual" actions. Often when I see rubbish lying somewhere, I pick it up and dispose it. The man answered:

"Good on you! **You know, people who selflessly recycle garbage and make the world even just a little better, are blessed.**"

Wow, I felt these words.

The man began to tell me about a place just around the corner, less than five minutes away. He said that since he entered this place for the first time, he believed in miracles again. He asked me if he could show it to me and because it was so close, I agreed.

We walked only a few streets and continued talking. He told me that in this place, every morning and every afternoon, food was distributed free of charge to people who depend on it. If they can, they give an amount for it as a donation. He invited me to come back the next morning and to have something. Or to read in one of the books that are also available there.

We went a bit further, he greeted some people along the way, probably his friends, and I was not yet aware of his true intention. He never asked me for money and was just as friendly when I told him that I was tired and would like to go back to the hotel. Tomorrow I would go to this place, I was very sure of it and also told him so. Our paths separated until I lost sight of the short-haired, white-bearded man.

The next morning I woke up early and of course liked to see this place. I was not hungry, just interested in what to explore there that the man was so enthusiastic about.

When I entered the street of the place, I saw him. Far away, I seemed to recognize the man from yesterday. He just left the place. I raised my arms and waved them, waved to him - he did not see me. I shouted his name, which he had mentioned to me yesterday, although I did not like to be too loud either, maybe I just misconceived myself. No reaction.

By the time I arrived at the place, he had already disappeared to the other direction.

I entered the premises. There were a few shelves of books and a buffet from which some people were taking food. In the background they slightly played mantra music and the general mood was thoughtful and full of gratitude.

A man at the entrance approached me and invited me to eat something as well. I refused thankfully because I felt that there were more indigent people than me. Some of the people surrounded a statue. They laid down flowers as a sign of gratitude around the statue, kissed the statue, and walked around it in circles with mumbling mantras and words of gratitude. When I got a clear view of the statue, my breath stopped. That was the man!

The man I talked to yesterday! The same short hair and the same white three-day stubble beard! Also on the walls hung pictures of him. This definitely had to be him!

I went to the shelves with books. I opened the one, that spoke most to me. I browsed over some pages and got stuck on a chapter:

"Sai Baba appeared in the form of a dog."

I read on the chapter and it was about Sai Baba coming to one in various forms. In this story he came to the author in the form of a dog.

I kept skimming and thinking to myself, what a great man to generously distribute food to people.

On the last page I found the years when Sai Baba had lived -

He was for more than 30 years dead.

# Categorie Modus Vivendi

… because honesty lasts the longest.

Give

Just be generous with what you have. What you give away returns in multitude. The more you give, the more you get.

Robert Kiyosaki

Imagine!

Imagine you are playing in a play and you are playing a role and you are aware, all the time, that you are playing a role. It is just a role that you are playing. You also play a role now, but you forgot that you are playing a role. You think that your body, the way it looks now, how it appears, what it does, were real, and you put all your energy into this game of playing that role. If you only were to put your energy into finding the self you have always been in reality!

Robert Adams

To simply be.

I always thought one has to have a goal, something to be focused on. However, I realized that life is much easier and way more enjoyable for me when I just sit back, let everything happen and enjoy the show. I embrace everything God gives me in my life and I play with that.

Sascha Të Light

A good traveler has no plans and no destination.

Lao Tzu

Enjoy.

Life is not a problem to be solved, it is a reality to be enjoyed.

Buddha

It passes…

There is the story of a student coming to a Zen master. He confesses to the Master, that he has such great difficulties in meditation. His back hurts, his legs hurt and every now and then he would even fall asleep. "It passes", says the Zen Master. Weeks later, the student returns and is in complete euphoria. He is doing so well, the student reports. He is awake, full of peace and joy and completely in presence. To which the Master replies: "It passes".

From Japan

The soft overcomes the hard, the weak triumphs over the strong.

Lao Tzu

Be water, my friend!

Bruce Lee

Light and Love.

Love - Everything and Everyone – That is the core intention. Words become secondary. The innermost principle of life is how we make others feel, which feelings others feel through our being. Feelings of uniqueness, of joy, of compassion, of serenity, of being enough, of being recognized, of being loved is that, which remains.

Sascha Të Light

To live inner freedom through forgiveness

To forgive has an enormously liberating effect. As we hold on to the attitude that others have hurt us, the tendency to be less cheerful and benevolent nor good-natured, develops – with the result that our peace of mind is gone, we no longer sleep soundly, and eventually our physical well-being may be impaired. However, when we are able to forgive those who have done us trouble, the feeling of inner peace and well-being automatically arises, which allows us to live on in harmony.   *

Dalai Lama

\* Forgiveness is not something that must necessarily happen in the presence of the other person or to the recognition that he or she was right. It is something you do for yourself, with the consequence of being emotionally free.

To be curious

I have no special talent, I am just passionately curious.

Albert Einstein

To know one's purpose

Many believe that they have a certain purpose, a definite one for life. This does not apply to everyone. It is true that before our incarnation we settle on a contract for this lifetime, which for many consists in simply "being". To simply be, as they are, is enough. Some people do not have to do more than that. They are generators of positivity. Their energy and aura and attitude to life alone is a beacon for others.

Dolores Cannon

As soon as something stops being fun, I think the time has come to move on. It is not the purpose of life to not be happy. This would not be a good way to live life.


Richard Branson

I would like to pay special attention to this quote from Richard Branson. It seems so obvious and simple, and yet it is not easy for many to let go and to move on. This is because this first step is not an easy one. Life runs habitually, money flows - and now, giving up everything? To break out of this habitual situation requires courage. And trust. Trust in life, and/or God, that it is always there, to support, and that it awakens certain feelings and inclinations within us, for a reason. Life will continue and it will always be there for us. Again and again there are going to be new and different ways to earn money and to live a happy life. The knowledge and deep understanding of this is gained through the experience of taking this step. What supposedly holds you back, is to let go of and to bravely walk the way, even if it appears uncertain at first.

"Those who prefer security over freedom will never be truly free."

Aristoteles

It is the case that there are certain fundamental rules and principles to life, which simply are. If you live in accordance with these regulations, the easier, more pleasant and harmonious your perceived quality of life. The first step is to know these and the second is to live as best as possible in accordance to these. The positive application leads to a pure and clear karma, infringes lead to a karma – burden. Life is realized as a mirror and reflection of the balance sheet of one's karma. The thoughts and feelings that predominate in the individual human being are the result of the individual karma-balance. The more ethically noble one acts, the purer one's karma, the freer one's life. There are ways to cleanse one's karma positively:

1. Service to others - generosity, goodwill, philanthropy

Prosperity is the consequence of the "empleasurement" of the quality of life of as many living beings as possible in the most effective and profound way.

Speak about and do to others only what should be said about/done onto yourself.

## 2. Avoiding actions contrary to the regulations of life

These are four of the major acts "against-life":

smoking

drinking alcohol

any intake or administration of poison

The killing of any form of life, be it human, animal, insect, plant – in relation to one's situation of life. Any involvement in this process must be omitted.

# 3. Meditation

Strength is to be found in stillness.

And while you adhere to these three basic principles, the permanent execution of these ten fundamental, noble virtues leads you to live life in a very special way:

# The Ten Noble Virtues

**Responsibility**
(Conscientiousness, Discipline)

**Godliness**
(Well-intentionedness, Philanthropy)

**Optimism** (Joyfulness, Cheerfulness)

**Sincerity** (Heed, Respect)

**Truthfulness** (Punctuality, Accurateness)

**Integrity** (Courage, Trust)

**Serenity** (Patience, Lightness)

**Sociability** (Interest, Togetherness)

**Kindness** (Sense of family, Sexuality)

**Growth** (Betterment)

**Others** (Simplicity, Gratitude, Appreciation, ...)

I recommend writing down these ten noble virtues and to visibly anchor them into your life, where they meet with your attention frequently. Internalize these virtues, make them the ethos of your life, realized in every word, in every deed.

# Categorie Water, Diet and Knowledge

… because this is what makes life effervesce.

Water is not equal to water

Water is not equal to water. Water is diverse, a mystical element of life that has not yet been fully understood. It makes a difference whether you drink water from the tap or from a bubbling, natural spring. The second is alive. And so one's life is more energetic, vital, healthier. Under normal circumstances, I am drinking only spring water.

Sascha Të Light

Light is everything

Everything is a form of light. We are light beings and function more efficiently the more light energy we consume. The question is, which foods provide the most potent light energy? These are the fruits, vegetables, nuts and seeds. A raw plant-based diet is the most illuminating diet on earth.

Nikola Tesla

The survival

Nothing will increase people's health and the chance of survival on Earth as much as the transition to a vegetarian diet.

Albert Einstein

The    fortune    of    a    living    diet

For verily I say to you, he who kills,
kills himself, and he who eats of the
flesh of slain animals, eats of the
body of death. But I say to you, kill
neither man nor animal, nor the food
that takes up your mouth. If you kill
your food, the dead food will also
kill you; if you eat living food, it will
enliven you.

Jesus Christ

The animal is YOU!

May all beings live happily, and to none may a calamity be met! May our whole lives help others. Every being shies away from torment, and everyone loves his life. Recognize yourself in every being, and do not torment nor kill.

Buddha

Therefore raw

If you take an apple and put it in the ground, a tree grows out of it. If you take an apple and you cook it, then put it in the ground, it deteriorates, no tree. The process of cooking diminishes something essential, the chi, the life energy. That is why I eat raw.

Markus Rothkranz

## Optimal learning

In order to be able to learn optimally, one must give one's brain the optimal fuel for optimal functioning. This fuel is the omega-3 fatty acid. That is why I eat raw-plant-based and especially flaxseeds, daily.


Sascha Të Light

The source

The library has always been the most
interesting place for me! I am just so
curious, I love to know everything!


Dolores Cannon

To bring forth wisdom

Go inside yourself and get the knowledge out of your own self. You are the greatest book that has ever been and will ever be. All external instruction is in vain, as long as the inner teacher does not awaken. One must go to the book of the heart and open it up in order to be valuable.

Swami Vivekânanda

As children we learned to crawl

First we explored the functionality of our body – what a mysterious object! Standing on two legs? Creating sounds that others understand?
Puuh, with increasing practice and experience we have mastered this.

This was followed by the training of the mind. What no one said, it never ends. It remains a constant and always lasting, curious and joyful exploration and investigation of the nature and functionality of our mind, our life, our being.

And we do it, we learn more and more, because with our insights we are a channel, a channel for our fellow human beings. For what we gained the honor of experience, we have experienced that in order to enrich the lives of all with it.


Sascha Të Light

# Categorie Finances

… for this is the reward for self-confident deeds.

Earning money

After leaving PayPal, I thought, "Okay, what are possible further challenges that are likely to affect the future of humanity?" I did not think, "How do I make money best?"


Elon Musk

Invest in education

You become what you learn. In the long run, education is more valuable than money. Curiosity and quick comprehension are extremely fast-advancing skills in today's fast-growing age.


Robert Kiyosaki

Rich is, who knows to have enough.

Lao Tzu

The key

Old ideas are the biggest obligation today, as times change very quickly. Efficient and innovative thinking and acting at the navel of time – this is the key.

Robert Kiyosaki

Maximize income

A person's merit is always in direct proportion to the degree of that person acquiring continuously and ever lastingly knowledge.

Sascha Të Light

Your energy is the only true currency

Treat your energy like you would money. Budget it, save it, find ways to increase it, invest it profitably. If you understand your energy like a form of currency, you will be surprised by how much this changes your reality. Our energy IS our true currency. Money is just symbolic for an exchange of energy. This is why you "pay" attention.

A New Me Apothecary & Wellness

The eighth wonder of the world

Compound interest is the eighth wonder of the world. Those who understand it, earn it. Those who do not, pay it.


Albert Einstein

Have less, be more

Gaining possessions means losing being. Therefore, the sorting out of the inessential is the core of all wisdom of life.

Lao Tzu

Focus on dividends

I built my investment strategy by my grandmother's very simple guideline: "Never sell the principle, only the dividend. And never never never ever invest in any asset that does not pay a dividend."

Kevin O'Leary

Secret to welfare

The great secret to wealth is to turn earnings into passive income as quickly as possible.


Robert Kiyosaki

# Categorie Wisdom

… because this is what remains.

What is the most important in the world?

It is the people, it is the people, it is the people.


Maori proverb

We are what we think

We are what we think. Everything we are originates from our thoughts. With our thoughts we shape the world. Tomorrow you will be what you are thinking today.

Buddha

Everything is energy

In order to understand the universe, think in terms of energy, frequency and vibration!

Nikola Tesla

Human nature is good.

Sascha Të Light

The core of religion

None of you is a person of faith
unless you like your brothers and
sisters to experience what you like
for yourself.

Mohamed

Everything you expect from others, do to them.

Jesus Christ

Believe yourself

Do not believe the scriptures, do not believe the teachers, do not believe me either. Believe only what you have carefully tested and recognized for your and the greater good.

Buddha

We are One

In the global community in which we live today, we are all interconnected to each other and interdependent – we all rely on each other. That is why it is no longer appropriate to divide our common world into 'us' and 'them'. The time has come for us all to think as one humanity.

Dalai Lama

We see things how we are.


Talmund

Axiom number 1

Behind every action is a positive intention, even if it is inappropriate or seems so in a certain context. Every person always makes the best choice of what is available to him/her at that given moment.

Core assumption 'Neurolinguistic Programming' (NLP)

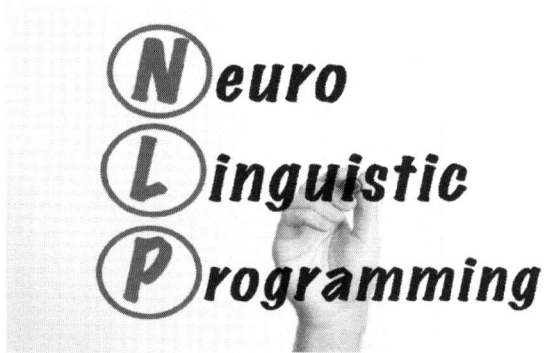

**Neuro Linguistic Programming**

Karma is real.

Dolores Cannon

The wise humans who realize that consciousness within them is the same as the consciousness of all beings have attained eternal peace.

Upanishads

The moccasins

Never judge your neighbor until you have walked two moons in his moccasins.

Cheyenne Indian proverb

Visitors

We are all just visitors to this world and at this time. Our souls are only in transit. Our job here is to observe, to learn, to grow, to love and then to go home again.

Wisdom of the Aborigines

## After death

After we move from the experience of this lifetime to the other side, we analyze it. We examine all our actions and statements, not only from our own point of view, also from the point of view of the other person involved. This is not always easy to see for many. I think that if we were all aware of this perspective in our communication, we would all be gentler, more benevolent and kinder with each other.


Dolores Cannon

Be brave

Be brave enough to do what your head tells you. Listen to your heart. Never say never.


Justin Bieber

The fact that Justin Bieber is among humanity's greatest geniuses may surprise some. He stands for the new, confident way of paying attention to inner feelings. While feelings were a lesser-regarded construct 50 years ago, they have made more inroads into people's lives in recent years. Many are recognizing now that we humans are constantly evolving, which is very much connected to our feelings in the current process of development.

It is well known that intuition, the gut feeling and the "seventh sense" have always been an important part of the human organism and our decision-making. It just is very recently that the inner state of affairs has been addressed so openly and courageously, as Justin Bieber's quote represents it. It always leads to a deeper connection between the participants when things that are present in the inner world are addressed in a meek and respectful way. It has also been a common Buddhist practice for centuries to include the heart for leadership in important life decisions. Here is a wonderfully simple and reliable technique, which provides deep and quick clarity when one does the following:

If a decision has to be made, one can

(1) sit down in peace, (2) go within, (3) place your right hand on your heart and (4) ask precise questions related to the decision.

Such as: Should I choose this option? What is the appropriate amount for this investment?

It is impressive with which accuracy the heart provides precise answers. The answers simply appear inside and are always correct.

"Do what you feel in your heart to be right."

# The Digression of Happiness

The purpose of life is to be happy. This is what all the people of the world have in common – the inner inclination to lead a happy life. Many believe that happiness can be found outside of us in materialistic things, while it truly is flowing basically from within, from the compassion and benevolence for our fellow human beings.

Dalai Lama

*Being happy is not a goal that is achieved at any particular point with a certain circumstance or object. Being happy is the way to life. You come to the realization and decide to simply be happy.*

Carlos Slim

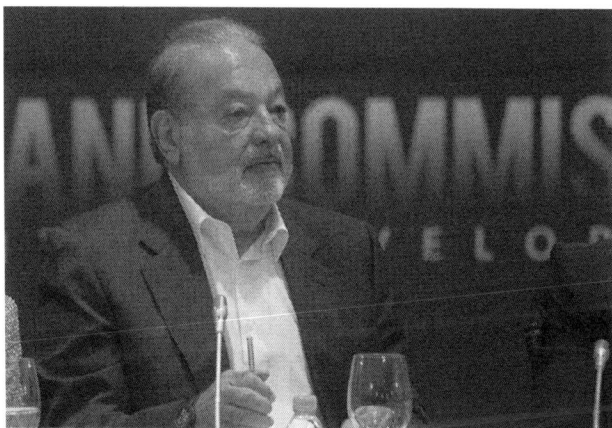

It is fascinating that these words come from Carlos Slim, one of the wealthiest persons in the world. He hits the essence of living a happy life to its core. It should be noted here that this does not only apply to the adjective of a 'happy' life. 'Happy' can be replaced by all adjectives and his statement is just the same. For example 'rich'.

*Being rich is not a goal that is achieved at any particular point with a certain circumstance or object. Being rich is the way to life. You come to the realization and decide to simply be rich.*

There is no number from which you are 'rich'. Examples of why you are 'rich' can always be found in every situation of life. You recognize, understand and decide to simply be rich. And life is always confirming our inner attitudes in the world outside of us. First the thought, the 'Be', then in the course of the realization over time, with patience, more and more the 'Have' is being manifested.

'Being' – 'Acting' - 'Having' – this is the course of life and the process of creation and realization.

# Enlightenment

… because this is what illuminates us all.

From discourse flows knowledge,

From knowledge flows understanding,

And from understanding flows Enlightenment.

Maori proverb

The carpenter works the wood. The archer bends the bow. The sage shapes itself.

Buddha

Promote, entertain and practice only the highest ideals in your life and be continually striving to make your lived ideals even more ideal. This is enlightenment and enlightening living.

Sascha Të Light

And finally, in deep deep gratitude, appreciation and connectedness to my friend Tonino, one of the warmest souls I have ever met:

From the moment ...

… fresh and newborn.

Yes free! Free from everything. What else is there? Simply to be. Let everything happen and rejoice in the moment, the present moment. I know nothing and that is all. I know that noThing and everything is contained within it and yet it is a mystery. How can this be, and how can it be?

Dual means separation. Being one is the most profound thing that has ever happened to me, but there was no one left who could experience it. Suddenly recognizing to be aware of one's own self. A message addressed to oneself. I am home, I have always been! I love myself, so I love you too! You

Antonino S. Yogonda

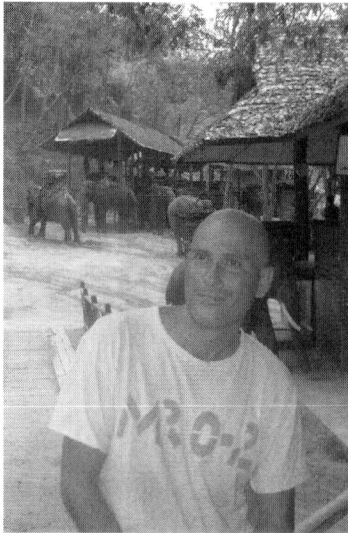

In eternal gratitude for your feedback/your opinion/your review:

https://www.amazon.com/dp/B08NRLJBRX

Also published by Freiheit.
JETZT!: (Freedom.NOW!)

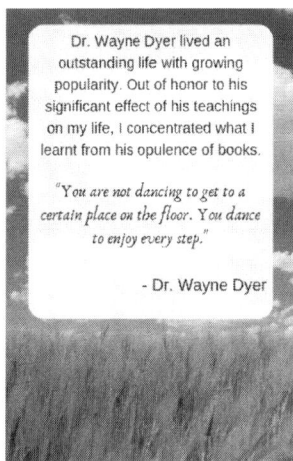

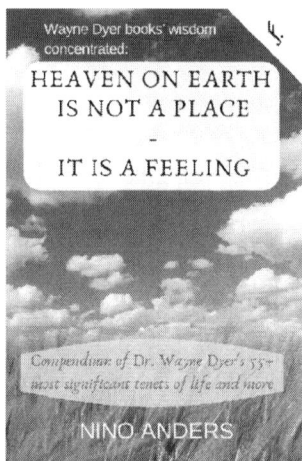

Nino Anders **Heaven on Earth is not a place – It is a Feeling**

Paperback: 8.99 Euro
Kindle eBook: 3.29 Euro

Dr. Wayne Dyer was an extraordinary person. With his teachings he inspired & enriched the lives of millions of people.

Choose to live heaven on earth by applying his 55+ highest ideas of wisdom to your life + PLUS the 3 moving farewell speeches of his daughters Saje, Skye and Serena, illustrating how Wayne lived his teachings in everyday life.

Amazon page:

https://amzn.to/2Ld6evH

Sascha Të Light - **How To Be Rich And Free Now** - Apply Just 5 Simple Eternal Money Generating Essentials

Paperback: 4.99 Euro
Kindle eBook: 2.99 Euro

There are basic principles, the 5 Simple Eternal Money Generating Essentials, which guarantee the amassment of wealth when one adheres to them. This precise quintessence presents them to enable every dear reader exuberant profits and freedom. Financial freedom is available to all of us, claim yours now.

Amazon page:

https://www.amazon.de/dp/1656907 410

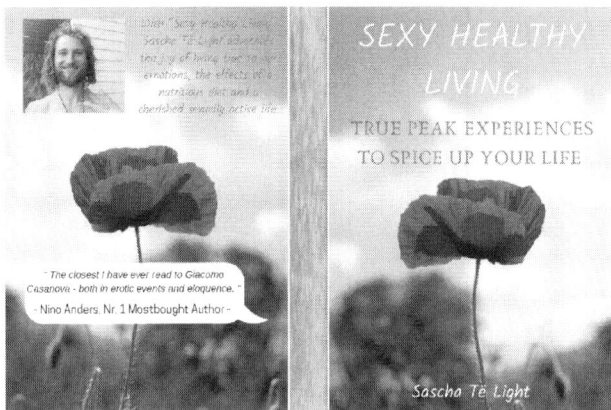

Sascha Të Light - **SEXY HEALTHY LIVING** - True Peak Experiences To Spice Up Your Life


Hardcover: 18.99 Euro

Taschenbuch: 12.99 Euro

Kindle eBook: 5.99 Euro

This book is an autobiographical and illustrated masterpiece of Sascha Të Light living fully during fifteen months in New Zealand. It is sharing openly very intimate revelations and stimulates with great eloquence.

Amazon page:
https://amzn.to/384s4gq

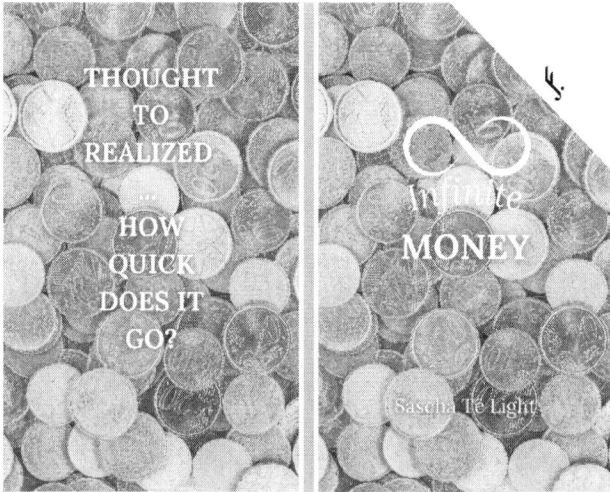

[Eng] Sascha Të Light – **Infinite MONEY** – How Quick Does It Go?

Kindle eBook: 142.99 Euro

Paperback: 224.99 Euro

Hardcover: 24.90 Euro

Thank you for your attention.

From now to Infinite MONEY in … days!

How few do you think it takes?

This book has not been written purely about Money. This book is about the freedom of humanity. There are laws which govern life - granting opulence to devotees. They are easy, plain and simple - everyone can understand and apply them.

It is time for you to prosper tremendously now.

* All remunerations of this book are being donated. The author has very much more money than enough any way

Amazon – page: https://amzn.to/3qJI3Gv

In eternal gratitude for your
feedback/your opinion/your review:

https://www.amazon.com/dp/B08NRL
JBRX

# **Credits for pictures**

Khalil Gibran

https://commons.wikimedia.org/wiki/File:Gibran_Khalil_Gibran.jpg

Albert Einstein

https://commons.wikimedia.org/wiki/File:Albert_Einstein_colourised_portrait.jpg

Jesus Christ

https://www.flickr.com/photos/vintage_illustration/46761047401

Robert Adams

https://commons.wikimedia.org
/wiki/File:Robert_Adams_-
_Los_Angeles_-
_early_1990s.jpg


T.S. Eliot

https://commons.wikimedia.org
/wiki/File:TS_Eliot.jpg


Huang Po

https://en.wikipedia.org/wiki/H
uangbo_Xiyun#/media/File:Hua
ngpo-1-.gif

Thomas Merton

https://www.flickr.com/photos/jimforest/2055118984


Lao Tzu

https://www.flickr.com/photos/beautifulcataya/2149939820


Sai Baba

https://commons.wikimedia.org/wiki/File:Sai_baba_rare_original_PRINT.jpg

Robert Kiyosaki

https://commons.wikimedia.org
/wiki/File:Robert_Kiyosaki_by_
Gage_Skidmore.jpg


Buddha

https://www.piqsels.com/de/pu
blic-domain-photo-zabnf


Japan

https://www.flickr.com/photos/
dominicspics/5748711462

Bruce Lee

https://www.flickr.com/photos/l
ex/43855760

Dalai Lama

https://de.wikipedia.org/wiki/D
alai_Lama#/media/Datei:Tenzin
_Gyatso_-
_14th_Dalai_Lama_(2012).jpg

Richard Branson

https://commons.wikimedia.org
/wiki/File:Richard_Branson_20
00.jpg

Aristoteles

https://commons.wikimedia.org
/wiki/File:Kopf_des_Aristoteles
_1.j

Nikola Tesla

https://snappygoat.com/s/?q=be
stof%3ATesla+magnifying+trans
mitte

Swami Vivekananda

https://commons.wikimedia.org
/wiki/File:Swami-
vivekananda.jpg

Elon Musk

https://commons.wikimedia.org
/wiki/File:Elon_Musk_Royal_So
ciety.jpg


Kevin O'Leary

https://commons.wikimedia.org
/wiki/File:Kevin_O%27Leary_2
012.jpg


Maori People

https://commons.wikimedia.org
/wiki/File:New_Zealand_-
_Maori_rowi

Mohamed

https://commons.wikimedia.org
/wiki/File:Everybody_Draw_Mo
hammed_

NLP

https://www.flickr.com/photos/
91261194@N06/49722972643

Upanishads

https://deacademic.com/picture
s/dewiki/83/Sadu_Kathmandu_
Pashupatinath_2006_Luca_Gal
uzzi.jpg

Cheyenne Indian

https://commons.wikimedia.org
/wiki/File:Bayfield_county_IMG
_1612_red_cliff_wisconsin_34th
_powwow.JPG


Aborigines

https://commons.wikimedia.org
/wiki/File:Aborigines_Sydney_A
ustralia_-_panoramio_-
_Vinko_Rajic_(3).jpg


Justin Bieber

https://beruhmte-
zitate.de/autoren/justin-bieber/

Carlos Slim

https://commons.wikimedia.org
/wiki/File:Carlos_Slim_(856288
7176).jpg

Printed in Great Britain
by Amazon